DREAMLAND

Learn with
PHONICS

DOUBLE-LETTER VOWEL SOUNDS

BOOK 5

Author
Lata Seth

Published by

DREAMLAND PUBLICATIONS

J-128, KIRTI NAGAR, NEW DELHI - 110 015 (INDIA)
Ph. : 011-2543 5657, 2510 6050 Fax. : 011-2543 8283
E-mail : dreamland@vsnl.com
www.dreamlandpublications.com

Published in 2014 by
DREAMLAND PUBLICATIONS
J-128, Kirti Nagar, New Delhi - 110 015 (India)
Tel : 011-2510 6050, Fax : 011-2543 8283
E-mail : dreamland@vsnl.com, www.dreamlandpublications.com
ISBN : 978-93-5089-534-4
Printed by
Haploos Printing House

Preface

Phonics is a method of teaching how to read using the sounds that letters represent. This series is a set of 5 books beginning with sounds connected with 26 letters of the English alphabet, short and long vowels and progressing to letter blends. The series has been especially designed for young learners aged 3 to 7 to help them become good readers. Words represented with pictures enhance and encourage independent learning and strengthen the spelling skills. A variety of exercises and engaging activities offer essential practice and inspire young learners to test what they have learnt. These workbook-based phonics books are recommended for young learners as well as teachers and parents who want to teach their children the art of reading.

Contents

Order of Lessons

Introduction

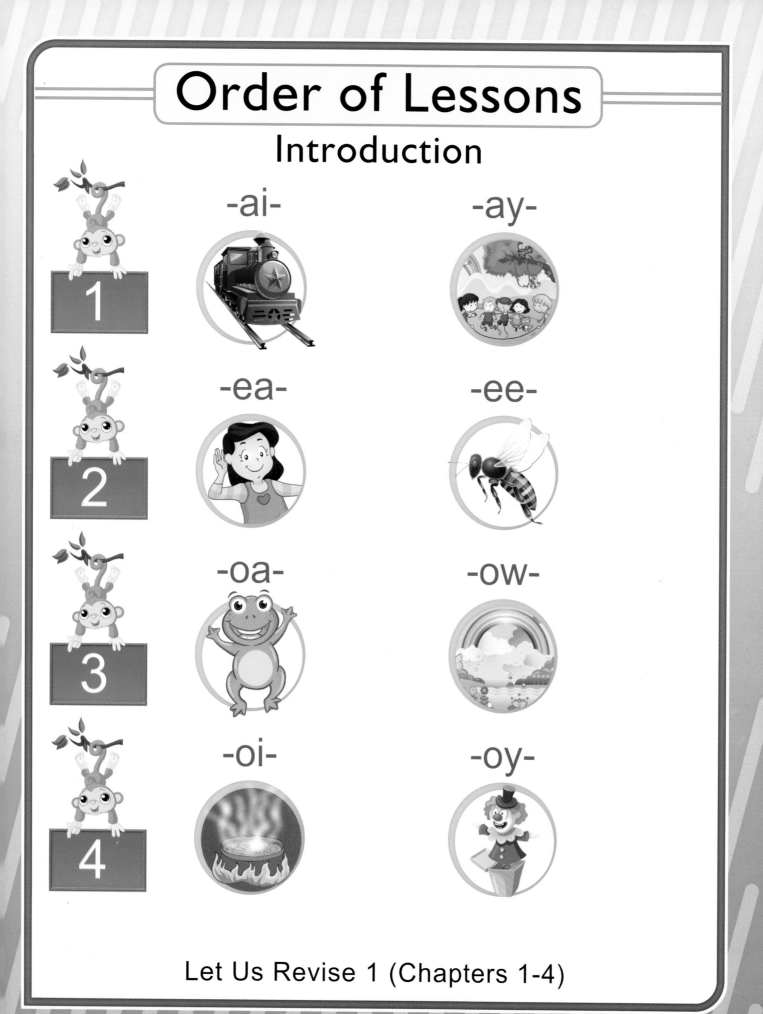

1

-ai-

-ay-

2

-ea-

-ee-

3

-oa-

-ow-

4

-oi-

-oy-

Let Us Revise 1 (Chapters 1-4)

Let Us Revise 2 (Chapters 5-8)
Let Us Review

Introduction

Hi! what are we going to learn in this book?

Well, in Book 4 we read about double-letter consonant sounds. In this book, we will learn double-letter vowel sounds. Some examples of double-letter vowel sounds are ai, ea, ee, oa. As you can see, there are two vowels here. These pairs say the name of the first vowel.

1 Sounds of Two-vowel Blends

-ai- -ay-

Let us learn the sounds of two-vowel blends -ai- and -ay-. Did you know that -ai- and -ay- make the same sound?

Read loudly and listen to the sounds.

ai

p + ai + l = pail

ay

h + ay + = hay

Here are some more new words for you.

ai

rain train wait

ay

play pray tray

Time to Solve

Say the name of each picture. Read the words and circle the word that names the picture. Write the word under the picture.

rain   train   pray   hay   pail   wait

rain

play   tray   wait   train   pray   play

   Write two more words for each sound.

ai
train

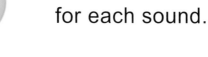

ay
hay

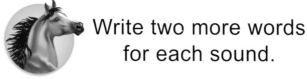

Betty wants to collect all the shells that have the -ay sound. Help her collect the shells circling those shells.

tray

train

pray

wait

hay

pail

play

Say the name of each picture. Then complete the words writing the missing letters.

hay

tr____

w____t

p____

l____r____n

pr____

Look at the pictures and find their names in the crossword.

p	a	i	l	i	t	a	y
l	g	w	a	p	r	a	y
a	r	i	y	l	a	h	a
y	y	t	a	y	i	a	y
p	l	r	a	i	n	t	g
a	y	t	i	a	y	r	a

Help Sally colour the shapes in blue which have the -ai- sounds.

play

rain

hay

wait

train

Fill in the missing word looking at the picture for clue.

Sam is going to _____.

I like going by _____.

Jenny has cookies on the _____.

It is going to _____ today.

Read the sentences / phrases
and match them to the pictures.

The pail is in the rain.

They wait for the bus.

The train is grey.

Children play on the hay.

Tick the sentence that
describes the picture.

☑ He waits for the train.

☐ He waits for the bus.

☐ The pail is on the hay.

☐ The pail is on the grass.

☐ The children pray.

☐ The children play.

Read the sentences. Find out the -ai- and -ay- words. Circle them. Then write them under the correct headings.

1. The train is late.

2. The girl loves to play.

3. John is carrying a tray of food.

4. The cat is getting wet in the rain.

5. I went to fetch a pail of water.

6. The children pray in the church every day.

ai	ay
train	

Story Time

Read this story aloud.

Sight Words — it, is, down, she

It is a cloudy day.
Polly waits for the train.

Polly sits down on the hay.
She carries a pail.

Soon, it rains.
Poor Polly is wet.

Luckily, the train comes along. Polly
climbs the train and goes away.

Time to Chant

Chhuk, chhuk, chhuk, comes the train,

Chhum, chhum, chhum, it's going to rain.

Clap, clap, clap, children play,

Tap, tap, tap, they jump on hay.

Hot, hot, hot, cakes on tray,

Give me some, to Mama I pray.

Do at Home

Fill in the blanks. Use the words from the box. Then rewrite the sentences.

pray	rain	tray	train	pail

1. The kids love to travel by _____.

_____

_____

_____

2. I _____ every day.

_____

_____

_____

3. The _____ is full of water.

_____

_____

_____

4. Mary is keeping cookies on the _____.

_____

_____

_____

5. The elephant is enjoying the _____.

_____

_____

_____

2 Sounds of Two-vowel Blends

-ea- -ee-

Let us learn the sounds of two-vowel blends -ea- and -ee-. Did you know that -ea- and -ee- make the same sound?

Read loudly and listen to the sounds.

ea

m + ea + t = meat

ee

b + ee + = bee

Here are some more new words for you.

e a

heat   sea   hear

e e

peek   tree   breeze

Time to Solve

Say the name of each picture. Read the words and circle the word that names the picture. Write the word under the picture.

bee   tree

hear   sea

peek   breeze

breeze   tree

meat   heat

hear   heat

Write two more words for each sound.

ea

ee

Fill in the missing word looking at the picture for clue.

The sun is giving out a lot of _____.

The _____ is very tasty.

The monkey is on the _____.

The _____ is on the beehive.

Say the name of each picture. Then complete the words writing the missing letters.

s ____

br __ ze

h ____ r

p ____ k

m ____ t

b ____

Fill in the blanks. Use the words from the box. Then rewrite the sentences.

| meat | tree | breeze | heat | bee |

1. There is a _____ on the flower.
_____
_____
_____

2. Mayra is enjoying the cool sea _____.
_____
_____
_____

3. The woman is cooking _____.
_____
_____
_____

4. The _____ is unbearable.
_____
_____
_____

5. The _____ is full of apples.
_____
_____
_____

Read the sentences / phrases and match them to the pictures.

They peek from behind the curtains.

The tree is swaying in the breeze.

She can hear what they are saying.

They are standing near the sea.

 Tick the sentence that describes the picture.

✓ The meat is on the shelf.

☐ The meat is on the table.

☐ The tree is outside the house.

☐ The tree is inside the house.

☐ The bee is on the wall.

☐ The bee is on the floor.

Read the sentence. Find out the -ea- and -ee- words. Circle them. Write them under the correct headings.

1. Harry is taking a peek from the tent.

2. She loves to hear pop music.

3. The dog is eating meat.

4. The bee is flying.

5. The sea is blue.

6. This is a big tree.

ea

_____
_____
_____
_____
_____
_____
_____

ee

_____
_____
_____
_____
_____
_____
_____

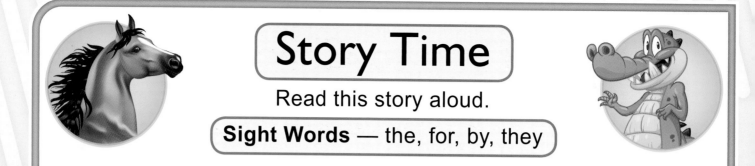

Story Time

Read this story aloud.

Sight Words — the, for, by, they

The children go
for a picnic by the sea.

A cool breeze is blowing. The
children enjoy the cool breeze.

They hear the sound of the waves
and swim in the blue sea.

Soon they feel hungry and eat
meat. They enjoy themselves.

Time to Chant

Busy bee, busy bee, resting in the heat,

Busy bee, busy bee, your buzz I can hear,

Go and rest on the tree, near the sea.

Do at Home

Fill in the blanks choosing the correct option.

There is a ship on the _____. (sea / tree)

The _____ is being roasted. (bee / meat)

The man is sweating in the _____.
(breeze / heat)

The _____ is being chopped. (tree / meat)

I love to _____ him talk. (hear / peek)

③ Sounds of Two-vowel Blends

-oa- -ow-

Let us learn the sounds of two-vowel blends -oa- and -ow-. Did you know that -oa- and -ow- make the same sound?

Read loudly and listen to the sounds.

oa

b + oa + t = boat

ow

r + ow + = row

Here are some more new words for you.

oa

coast

toad

soap

ow

snow

rainbow

pillow

Time to Solve

Say the name of each picture. Read the words and circle the word that names the picture. Write the word under the picture.

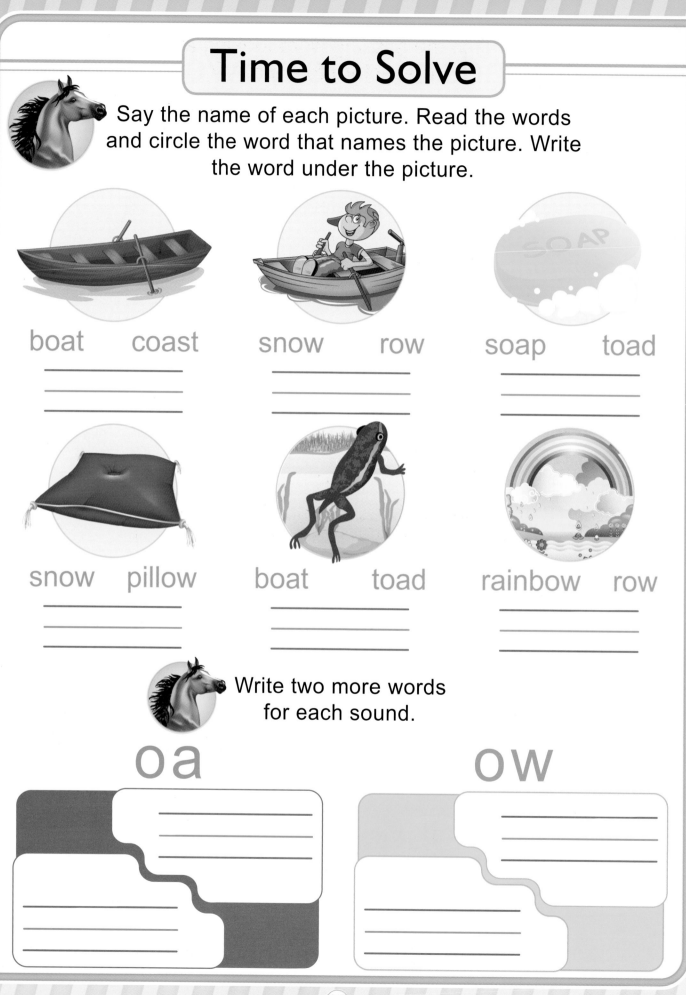

boat   coast

_____
_____
_____

snow   row

_____
_____
_____

soap   toad

_____
_____
_____

snow   pillow

_____
_____
_____

boat   toad

_____
_____
_____

rainbow   row

_____
_____
_____

Write two more words for each sound.

oa

_____
_____

_____
_____

ow

_____
_____

_____
_____

Fill in the missing word looking at
the picture for clue.

He owns a big _____.

The people have made the _____ dirty.

Wash your hands with _____.

The _____ is sitting on the rock.

Say the name of each picture. Then complete
the words writing the missing letters.

r _____

t ____ d

rainb____

s ____

p pill____

b ____ t

Fill in the blanks. Use the words from the box. Then rewrite the sentences.

rainbow	pillow	soap	snow	row

1. He loves to _____ the boat.

_____

_____

2. The _____ has a nice smell.

_____

_____

3. The trees are covered with _____.

_____

_____

4. The children are looking at the _____.

_____

_____

5. The girl has a pink _____.

_____

_____

Read the sentences / phrases and match them to the pictures.

The boat is brown.

The toad is on the pillow.

The soap is in the dish.

The old man is standing on the snow.

 Tick the sentence that describes the picture.

✓ The soap is on the pillow.

☐ The soap is on the toad.

☐ The toad is dancing.

☐ The toad is singing.

☐ The rainbow is colourful.

☐ The snow is colourful.

Read the sentences. Find out the -oa- and -ow- words. Circle them. Write them under the correct headings.

1. The sea coast is full of birds.

2. Always wash your hands with soap.

3. I love to see the rainbow.

4. This pillow is very soft.

5. This toad is big.

6. Children play in the snow.

oa

ow

Story Time

Read this story aloud.

Sight Words — the, in, to, his

The toad sees
the rainbow in the sky.

The toad wants to
sleep under the rainbow.

The toad takes his pillow to
sleep under the rainbow.

Suddenly, it begins to snow. The
toad comes back with the pillow.

Time to Chant

Row the boat Mr. Toad, take the boat to the coast,

See the rainbow in the sky, pretty colours up so high.

Do at Home

Fill in the blanks choosing the correct option.

There is a _____ in the pond. (boat / snow)

The _____ is made of cotton. (boat / pillow)

There is a _____ in the bathroom.
(toad / soap)

The _____ is being chased by a snake.
(toad / row)

I can see the _____ . (coast / rainbow)

4 Sounds of Two-vowel Blends

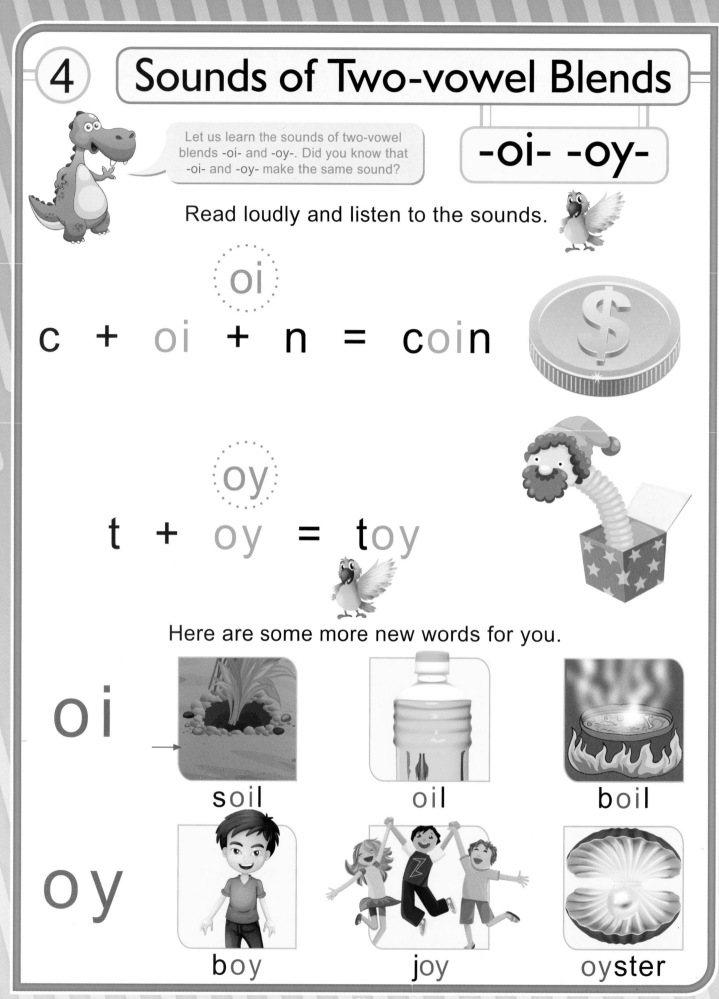

Let us learn the sounds of two-vowel blends -oi- and -oy-. Did you know that -oi- and -oy- make the same sound?

-oi- -oy-

Read loudly and listen to the sounds.

oi

c + oi + n = coin

oy

t + oy = toy

Here are some more new words for you.

oi

soil   oil   boil

oy

boy   joy   oyster

Time to Solve

Say the name of each picture. Read the words and circle the word that names the picture. Write the word under the picture.

boy   toy

_____

boil   coin

_____

joy   toy

_____

oyster   joy

_____

soil   boil

_____

coin   oil

_____

Write two more words for each sound.

oi

_____

oy

_____

Fill in the missing word looking at the picture for clue.

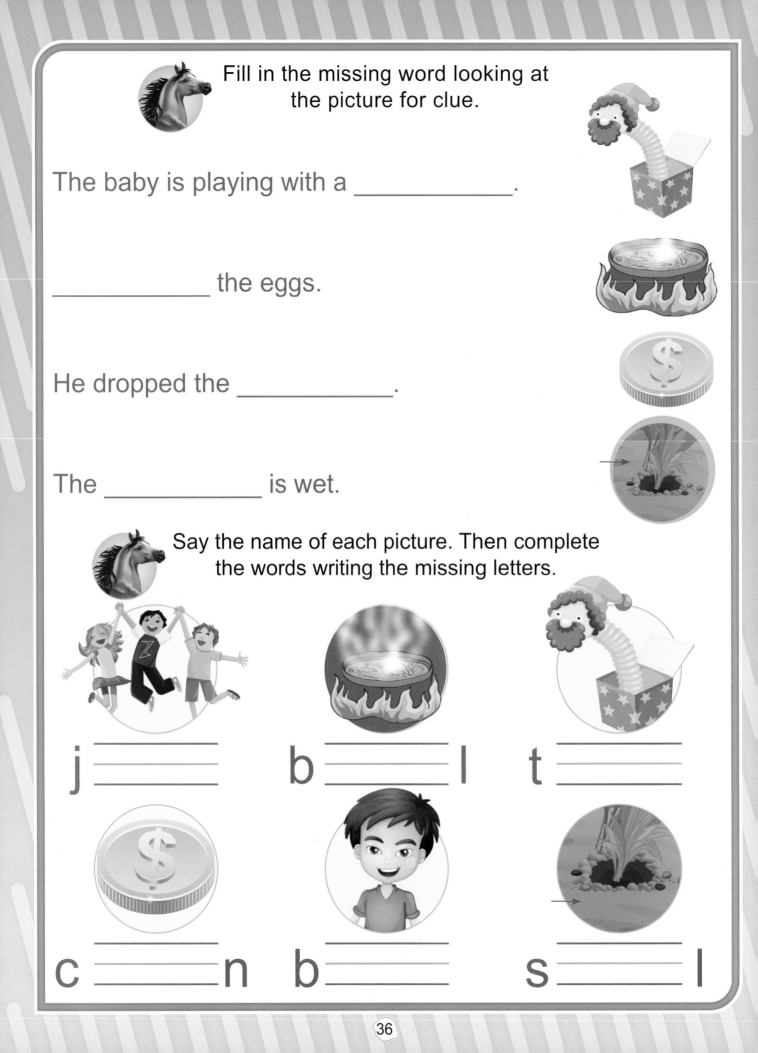

The baby is playing with a _____.

_____ the eggs.

He dropped the _____.

The _____ is wet.

Say the name of each picture. Then complete the words writing the missing letters.

j _____

b _____ l

t _____

c _____ n

b _____

s _____ l

Fill in the blanks. Use the words from the box. Then rewrite the sentences.

| toy | oil | coin | boil | boy |

1. Mary is playing with a _____.

_____

_____

2. _____ the milk.

_____

_____

3. The _____ rides a bicycle.

_____

_____

4. The _____ is in the bottle.

_____

_____

5. The _____ is shining brightly.

_____

_____

Read the sentences / phrases
and match them to the pictures.

The toy is red in colour.

The oil is on the road.

The oysters are on the plate.

The coin is on the table.

 Tick the sentence that
describes the picture.

☑ The coin is on the soil.

☐ The oil is in the soil.

☐ The boy has a toy.

☐ The boy has a coin.

☐ The oysters are boiling.

☐ The oil is in the bottle.

Read the sentence. Find out the -oi- and -oy- words. Circle them. Write them under the correct headings.

1. The coin is golden in colour.

2. The girl got a toy from her mother.

3. The man digs the soil.

4. The girl jumped with joy.

5. She is pouring oil from the bottle.

6. The boy is sad.

oi	oy
_____	_____
_____	_____
_____	_____
_____	_____
_____	_____

Story Time

Read this story aloud.

Sight Words — he, some, then

The boy is hungry.
He has a coin.

The boy buys some oysters.
He boils the oysters.

Then the boy fries
the oysters in the oil.

The boy enjoys
eating the oysters.

Time to Chant

Johnny boy, Tony boy, play with a toy

And have a lot of joy.

They find a coin and bring some oil.

Mama fry the eggs and keep them in a foil.

41

Do at Home

Fill in the blanks choosing the correct option.

The girl looks at the _____ in the shop. (toy / coin)

The _____ is wearing a green T-shirt. (boy / toy)

He sowed seeds in the _____ . (soil / oil)

She is putting _____ in the pan. (soil / oil)

He is full of _____ as he has passed the test. (boy / joy)

Let Us Revise 1

Chapters 1-4

Hi Friends! let us test what you have learnt so far.

Fill in the missing letters.
Then match the word to the picture.

p [ ] [ ] l

b r [ ] z e

t [ ] d

[ ] s t e r

See the picture and circle the correct word.

| wait | train | | boat | meat |

| row | toy | | boy | boil |

| toy | snow | | play | joy |

Tick the sentence that describes the picture.

☑ The boy has a pail.

☐ The boy has hay.

☐ The bee peeks from the window.

☐ The toad peeks from the window.

☐ The water is boiling.

☐ The oysters are boiling.

 Match the phrase to the picture.

Kids with hay and pail

Bee on a tree

Toad in a boat

Oyster in the oil

Look at the pictures for clues and then write
the name for each picture.

_____   _____   _____
_____   _____   _____

_____   _____
_____   _____
_____   _____

Fill in the blanks choosing the correct word
from the names written above.

The green _____ sat on the pail.

The _____ is late.

There are many fish in the _____ .

The boy sells _____ in the market.

The _____ is sitting on the flower.

Write the word for each picture.
Then find the words in the crossword.

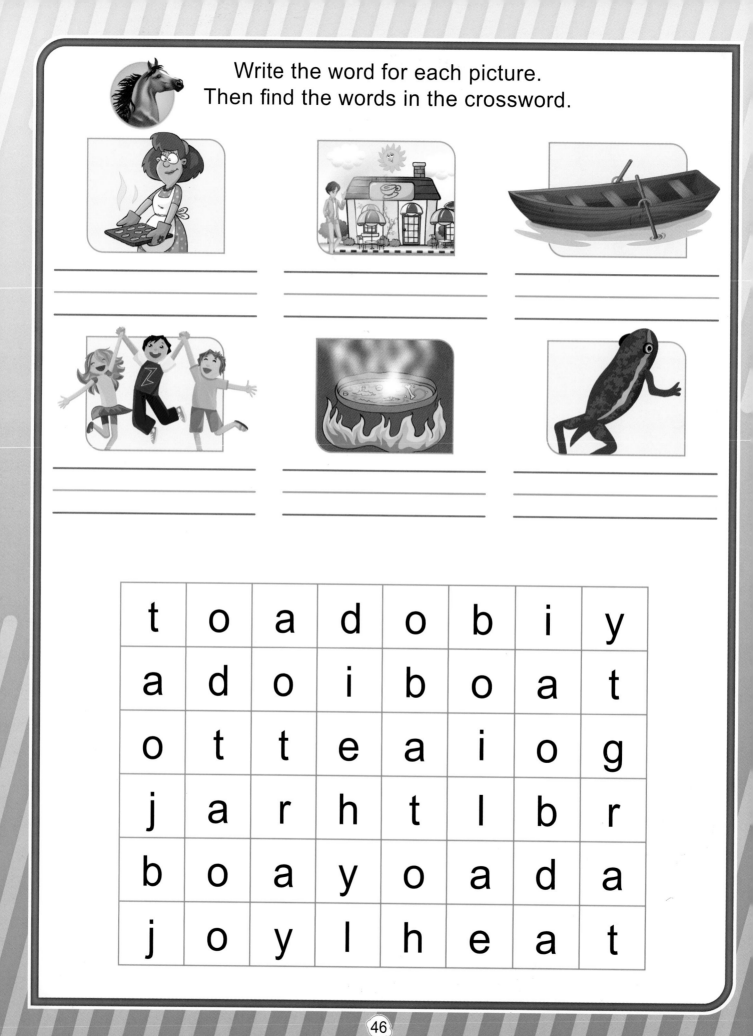

t	o	a	d	o	b	i	y
a	d	o	i	b	o	a	t
o	t	t	e	a	i	o	g
j	a	r	h	t	l	b	r
b	o	a	y	o	a	d	a
j	o	y	l	h	e	a	t

Fill in the missing words choosing the two-vowel blends from the box to complete each story.

-ai, -ay, -ea, -oy

The children pl__ in the hay.

They h__r the tr__n's sound.

They see the tr__n coming.

They are filled with j__ to see the tr__n. One b__ goes on the tr__n.

-oa, -ea, -ow

The man loves to r__ his b__t. He takes the b__t to the s__ every day. But today, there is sn__ everywhere. So the man does not r__ his boat.

5 Sounds of Two-vowel Blends

-ou- -ow-

Let us learn the sounds of two-vowel blends -ou- and -ow-. Did you know that -ou- and -ow- make the same sound?

Read loudly and listen to the sounds.

ou

m + ou + se = mouse

ow

ow + l + = owl

Here are some more new words for you.

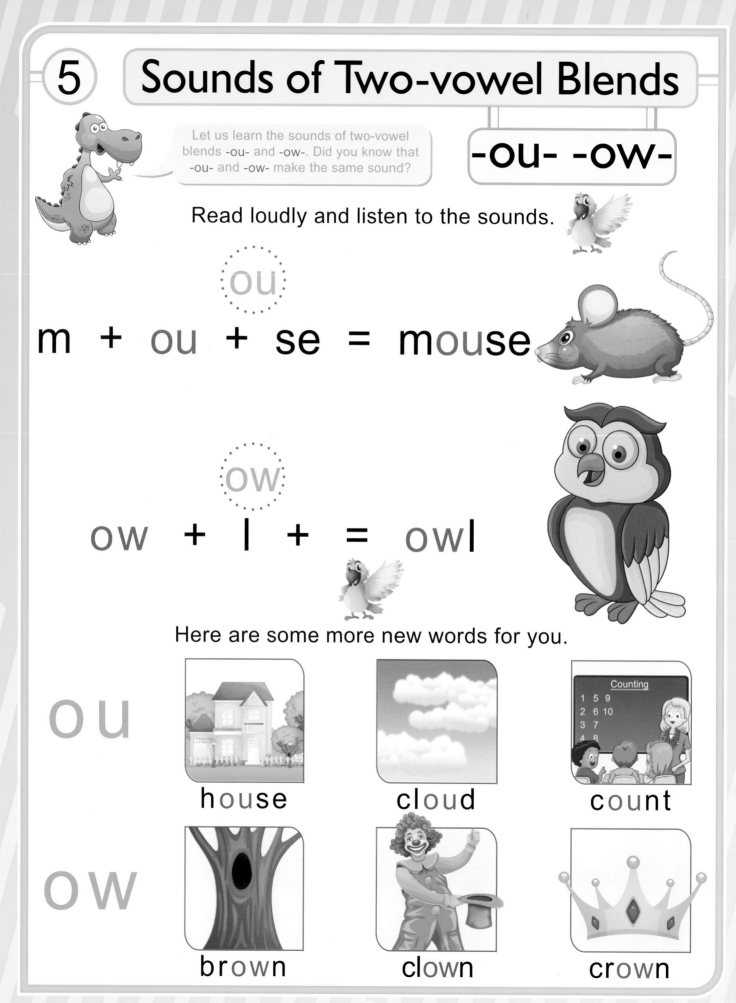

ou

house

cloud

count

ow

brown

clown

crown

Time to Solve

Say the name of each picture. Read the words and circle the word that names the picture. Write the word under the picture.

cloud   count

clown   owl

house   mouse

crown   clown

count   house

brown   crown

Write two more words for each sound.

ou

ow

Fill in the missing word looking at the picture for clue.

The _____ is very big.

The children clapped for the _____.

She loves to _____ the stars.

The box is _____ in colour.

Say the name of each picture. Then complete the word writing the missing letters.

____l   cr____n   c____nt

br____n   m____se   h____se

Fill in the blanks. Use the words from the box. Then rewrite the sentences.

mouse   house   clouds   crown   owl

1. The _____ is looking at the snake .
_____
_____
_____

2. The sky is covered with _____.
_____
_____
_____

3. The _____ is eating cheese.
_____
_____
_____

4. The queen wears a _____ .
_____
_____
_____

5. The _____ is very grand.
_____
_____
_____

Read the sentences / phrases and match them to the pictures.

The white clouds

The happy clown

The flying owl

The brown house

 Tick the sentence that describes the picture.

☐ The owl is in the house.

✓ The owl is outside the house.

☐ The mouse is brown.

☐ The mouse is grey.

☐ The clown is sad.

☐ The clown is happy.

Read the sentence. Find out the -ou- and -ow- words. Circle them. Write them under the correct headings.

1. The girl's dress is brown.

2. The clown has many rings.

3. The man has to count the apples.

4. The house has a big garden.

5. The crown has many diamonds on it.

6. The mouse is at the rooftop.

ou

_____

_____

_____

_____

_____

_____

ow

_____

_____

_____

_____

_____

_____

Story Time

Read this story aloud.

Sight Words — he, some, the

The mouse has some pieces of cheese. But he does not know how to count.

The mouse goes to the clown. The clown counts the pieces.

One, two, three ....
There are four pieces in all.

The mouse shares the cheese with the clown.

Time to Chant

A stout clown wears a crown, and dances up and down,

One, two, and three, he starts to count, the steps he mounts.

Brown mouse wears a gown, and goes to the town,

One, two, and three, she starts to count.

The cheese she gets on heavy discount.

Do at Home

Fill in the blanks choosing the correct option.

The _____ is on the tree. (owl / mouse)

The wall is painted in _____ colour. (brown / white)

The aeroplane is in the _____. (tree / clouds)

His job is to _____ money. (count / clown)

The king wears a _____. (cloud / crown)

6 Sounds of Two-vowel Blends

-oo- -oo-

Let us learn the sounds of two-vowel blends -oo- (long) and -oo- (short).

Read loudly and listen to the sounds.

oo

p + oo + l = pool

oo

c + oo + k = cook

Here are some more new words for you.

o o

moon food tooth

o o

book foot wood

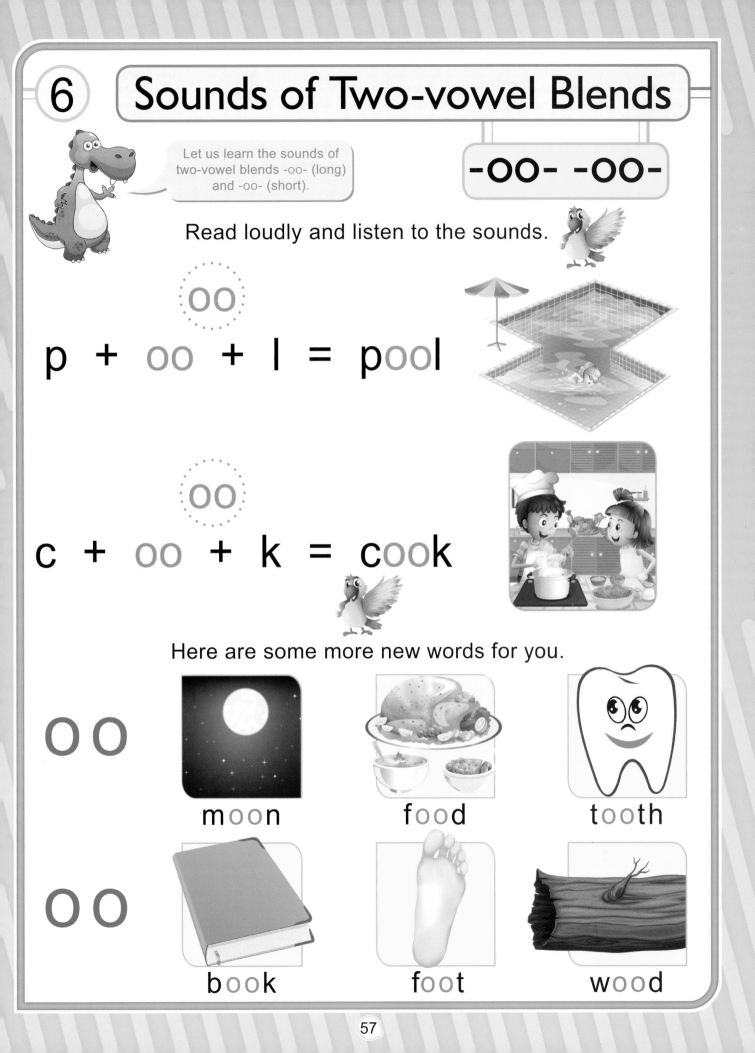

Time to Solve

Say the name of each picture. Read the words and circle the word that names the picture. Write the word under the picture.

wood   book   pool   food   moon   tooth

_____   _____   _____

wood   cook   book   cook   tooth   moon

_____   _____   _____

Write two more words for each sound.

oo

oo

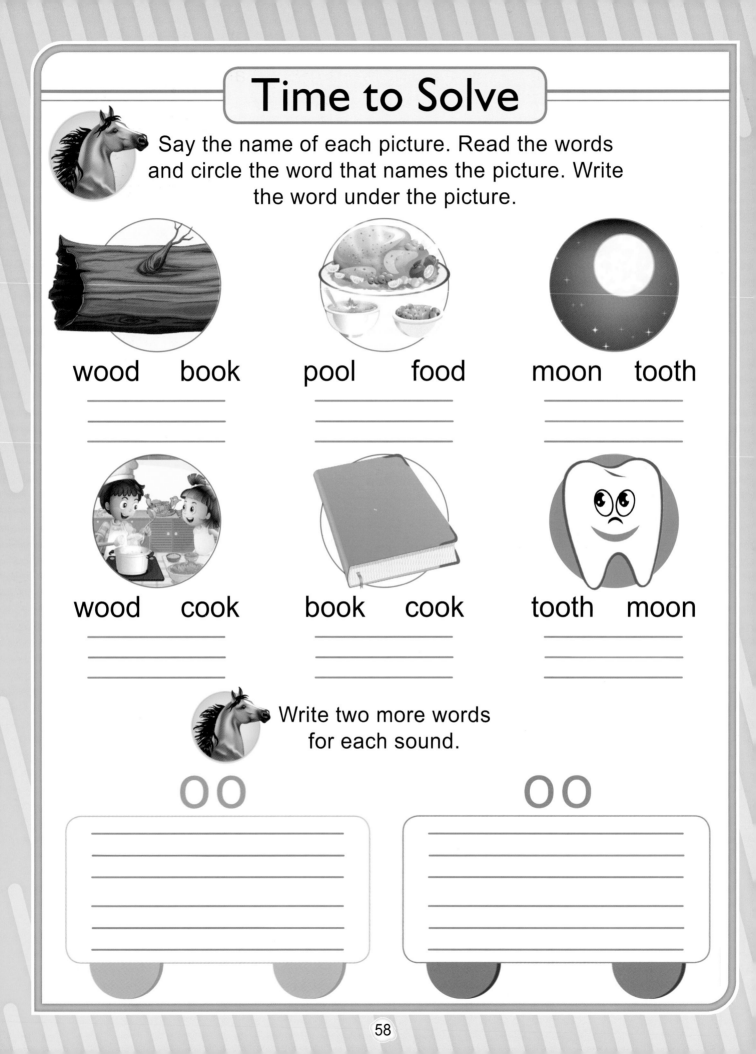

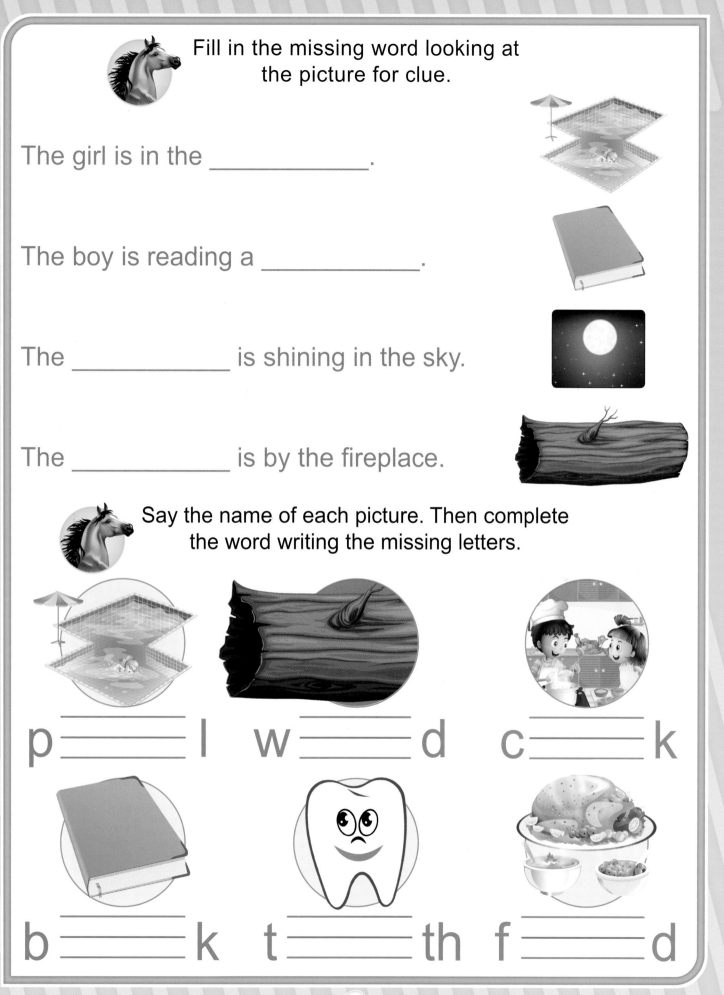

Fill in the missing word looking at the picture for clue.

The girl is in the _____.

The boy is reading a _____.

The _____ is shining in the sky.

The _____ is by the fireplace.

Say the name of each picture. Then complete the word writing the missing letters.

p ____ l   w ____ d   c ____ k

b ____ k   t ____ th   f ____ d

59

Fill in the blanks. Use the words from the box. Then rewrite the sentences.

| cook | food | moon | book | wood |

1. The _____ is round today .

_____

_____

_____

2. The girl loves to _____.

_____

_____

_____

3. This is an interesting _____.

_____

_____

_____

4. She brought _____ for the fireplace.

_____

_____

_____

5. The _____ is very hot.

_____

_____

_____

Read the sentences / phrases and match them to the pictures.

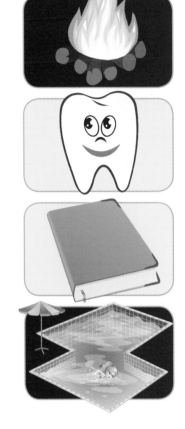

The blue pool

The thick book

The white tooth

The burning wood

 Tick the sentence that describes the picture.

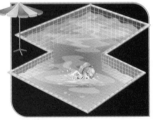

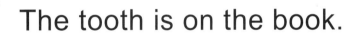 ✓ The tooth is on the book.

☐ The book is on the tooth.

☐ The moon is full.

☐ The pool is full.

☐ The book is red.

☐ The book is blue.

61

 Read the sentence. Find out the -oo- and -oo- words. Circle them. Write them under the correct headings.

1. The moon shines in the sky.

2. The book is on the table.

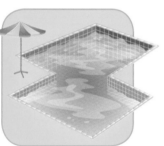

3. The tooth is yellow.

4. The wood is in the garden.

5. The pool is empty.

6. Mother loves to cook.

OO

OO

Story Time

Read this story aloud.

The boy has a broken tooth.

He keeps the tooth
under his pillow.

He dreams that the tooth-fairy
takes his tooth.

When he looks for the tooth, it is not
there. 'Who took the tooth?' he wonders.

Time to Chant

Mama loves to cook, she also writes a book,

Mama, please have a look, I have a broken tooth,

Look, look, near the brook, there is a rook, with some food,

He makes fun of my missing tooth.

Do at Home

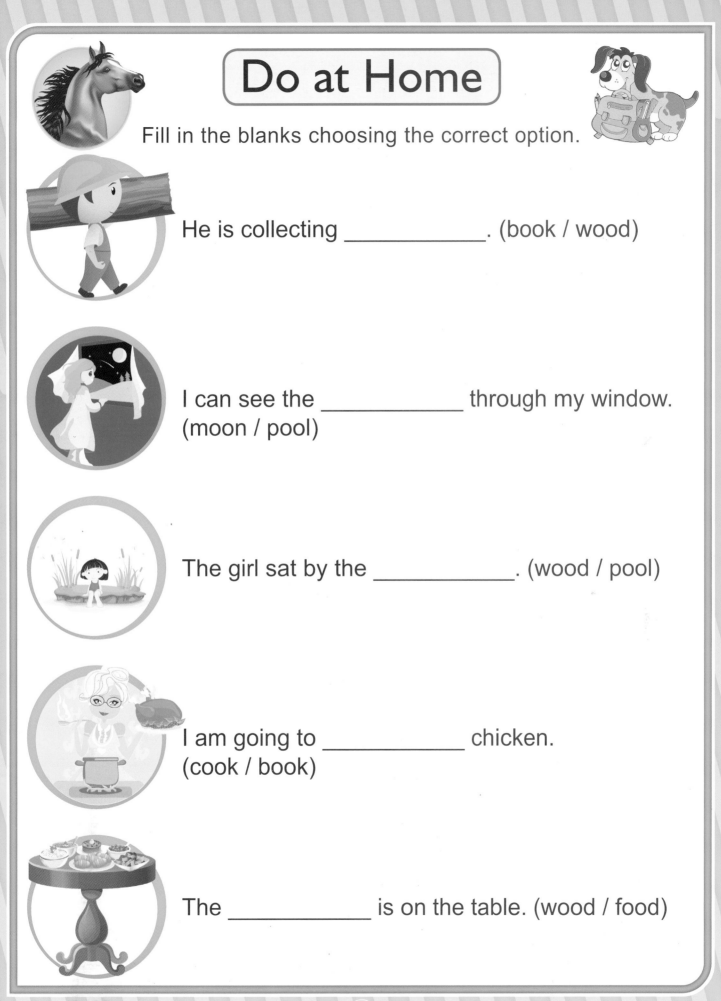

Fill in the blanks choosing the correct option.

He is collecting _____. (book / wood)

I can see the _____ through my window.
(moon / pool)

The girl sat by the _____. (wood / pool)

I am going to _____ chicken.
(cook / book)

The _____ is on the table. (wood / food)

7 Sounds of Two-vowel Blends

-ar- -or-

Let us learn the sounds of two-vowel blends -ar- and -or-. Did you know that -ar- and -or- make similar sounds?

Read loudly and listen to the sounds.

ar

f + ar + m = farm

or

f + or + t = fort

Here are some more new words for you.

ar

park   farmer   dark

or

horn   torch   sport

Time to Solve

Say the name of each picture. Read the words and circle the word that names the picture. Write the word under the picture.

dark   farm

horn   fort

farmer   farm

fort   torch

park   dark

horn   sport

Write two more words
for each sound.

ar

or

Fill in the missing word looking at
the picture for clue.

The _____ is full of flowers.

This _____ is very old.

The boy is very good in this _____.

This rhino has one _____.

Say the name of each picture. Then complete
the words writing the missing letters.

sp____t   f____mer   h____n

d____k   t____ch   p____k

Fill in the blanks. Use the words from the box. Then rewrite the sentences.

torch   fort   park   farmer   dark

1. This street is very _____.

_____
_____
_____

2. He goes for a walk in the _____ every day.

_____
_____
_____

3. The fire of this _____ is very bright.

_____
_____
_____

4. The _____ loves his animals.

_____
_____
_____

5. The fairy was kept locked in a _____.

_____
_____
_____

Read the sentences / phrases and match them to the pictures.

The old fort

The big horn

The beautiful park

The farmer with a hat

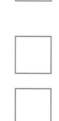 Tick the sentence that describes the picture.

☑ The farmer is old.

☐ The farmer is young.

☐ The fort is grey.

☐ The fort is blue.

☐ The park is dark.

☐ The farm is dark.

Read the sentences. Find out the -ar- and -or- words. Circle them. Write them under the correct headings.

1. There is a farm outside the city.

2. The runner always carries a torch with him.

3. This park is full of people.

4. He loves to play any kind of sport.

5. This farmer sells cheap vegetables.

6. The horn of a rhino is very expensive.

ar	or

Story Time

Read this story aloud.

Sight Words — he, his, and

A farmer visits a fort.
It is very dark inside the fort.

The farmer carries a torch.
He switches on his torch.

The farmer sees a shadow
in the fort and screams.

The farmer comes running out of
the fort. Whose shadow was it?

Time to Chant

The farmer in the farm, hears an alarm.

He goes to the fort, and lights the torch.

He sees a rhino, with one horn.

Do at Home

Fill in the blanks choosing the correct option.

There is a _____ up the hill. (fort / park)

There is a big apple tree in the _____.
(park / farm)

He searched for his pencil in the _____.
(dark / park)

She shone her _____ on the coin.
(horn / torch)

She is exercising in the _____.
(park / farm)

Sounds of Two-vowel Blends

-er- -ir- -ur-

Let us learn the sounds of two-vowel blends -er-, -ir- and -ur-. Did you know that -er-, -ir- and -ur- make the same sounds?

Read loudly and listen to the sounds.

er

d + an + c + er = dancer

ir

b + ir + d = bird

ur

f + ur = fur

Here are some more new words for you.

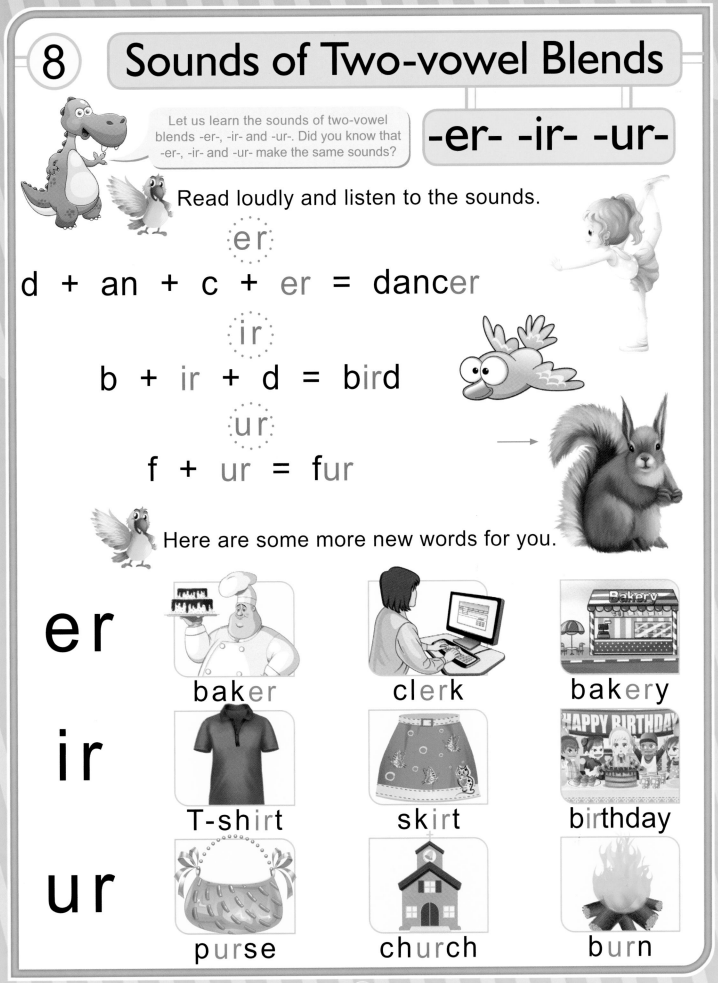

er	baker	clerk	bakery
ir	T-shirt	skirt	birthday
ur	purse	church	burn

Time to Solve

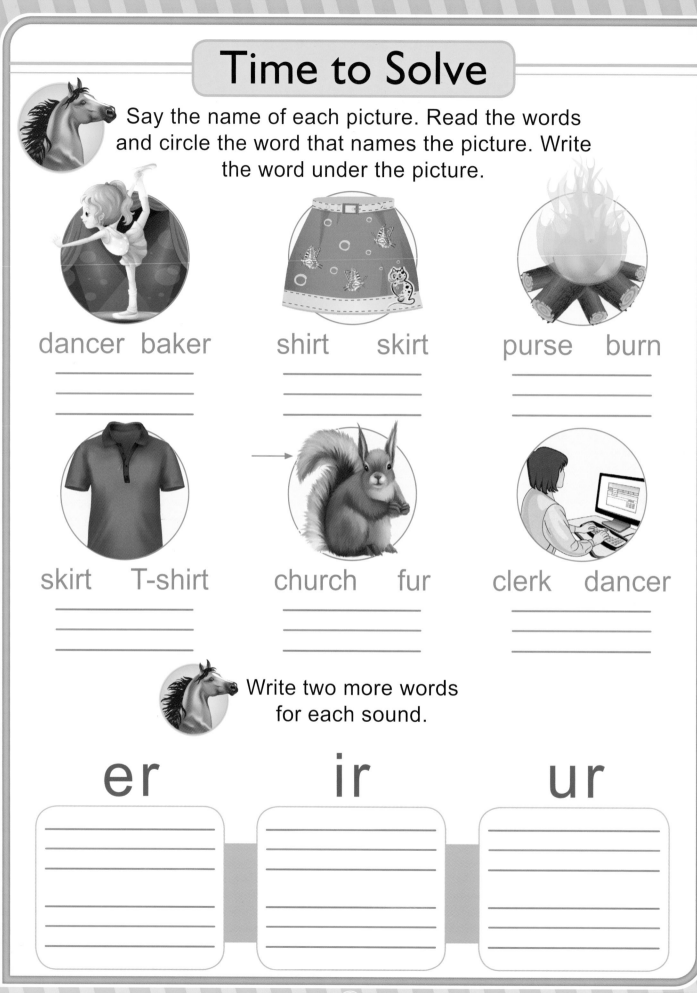

Say the name of each picture. Read the words and circle the word that names the picture. Write the word under the picture.

dancer baker

shirt   skirt

purse   burn

_____
_____
_____

skirt   T-shirt

church   fur

clerk   dancer

_____
_____
_____

Write two more words for each sound.

er

ir

ur

Fill in the missing word looking at
the picture for clue.

The _____ works very hard.

This _____ is sitting on the tree.

The _____ is on the table.

This _____ is red.

Say the name of each picture. Then complete
the words writing the missing letters.

T-sh___t   bak___y   f___

p___se   b___d   cl___k

Fill in the blanks. Use the words from the box. Then rewrite the sentences.

| dancer | birthday | purse | bakery | church |

1. The _____ near the street has good cakes.

_____

_____

_____

2. They are celebrating her _____ today.

_____

_____

_____

3. The man is going to the _____.

_____

_____

_____

4. The _____ won the competition.

_____

_____

_____

5. My _____ is empty.

_____

_____

_____

Read the sentences / phrases and match them to the pictures.

The pink fur

The small skirt

The pretty dancer

The big church

 Tick the sentence that describes the picture.

✓ The purse is red.

☐ The purse is green.

☐ The bird is sitting on the tree.

☐ The bird is sitting on the house.

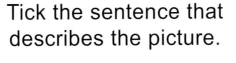

☐ The clerk is typing.

☐ The dancer is typing.

Read the sentences. Find out the -er-, -ir- and -ur- words. Circle them. Write them under the correct headings.

1. She bought a purse from the shop.

2. The birthday cake is made of chocolate.

3. The clerk is doing overtime.

4. The church is closed today.

5. The dancer performed badly yesterday.

6. The bird has made a nest.

er	ir	ur

Story Time

Read this story aloud.

Sight Words — it, is, down, she

It is Tom's birthday. His mother goes to the bakery.

She orders a big cake for her son. She pays money from her purse.

She goes to the church and prays for her son.

In the evening, Tom is happy to see a big birthday cake for him.

Time to Chant

The dancer dances, tap, tap, tap,

The children clap, clap, clap, clap,

The bird flies, flap, flap, flap,

Birthday time, clap, clap, clap.

Do at Home

Fill in the blanks choosing the correct option.

They are getting married in the _____.
(bakery / church)

The bear's _____ keeps it warm.
(fur / shirt)

The _____ baked some delicious cookies.
(baker / dancer)

The bear is wearing a _____ .
(T-shirt / torch)

He set the _____ free. (bird / shirt)

Let Us Revise 2

Chapters 5-8

Fill in the missing letters.
Then match the word to the picture.

		l

w		d

f		m

b	a	k		y

See the picture and circle the correct word.

fur   church   fort   torch

moon   pool   house   mouse

brown   clown   dancer   baker

84

Tick the sentence that describes the picture.

✓ The T-shirt is brown.

☐ The T-shirt is blue.

☐ The mouse is on the table

☐ The mouse is on the chair.

☐ The house is in the park.

☐ The house is in the farm.

 Match the phrase to the picture.

The burning wood

The busy clerk

The silver crown

The huge fort

Look at the pictures for clues and then write
the name for each picture.

_____   _____   _____
_____   _____   _____
_____   _____   _____

_____   _____
_____   _____
_____   _____

Fill in the blanks choosing the correct word
from the names written above.

The _____ is sitting on a tree.

The _____ is very funny.

The _____ has hot water.

There are many sheep in the _____.

The _____ is flying high in the sky.

Write the word for each picture.
Then find the words in the crossword.

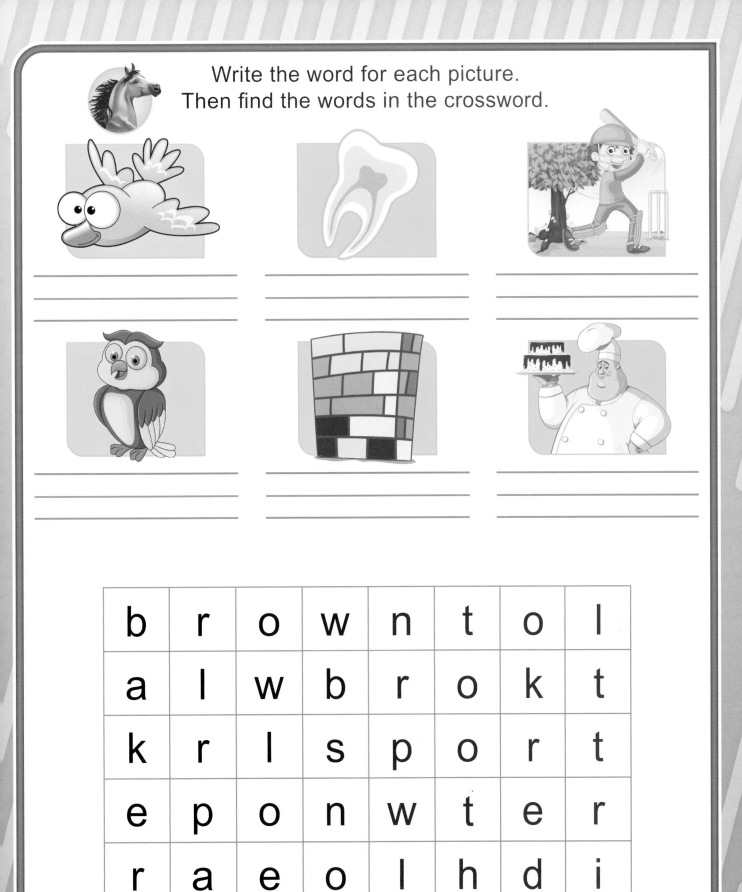

Fill in the missing words choosing the two-vowel blends from the box to complete each story.

ou, oo, ow

I live in a big h__se. There is a p__l in my h__se. I have a pet m__se also. I keep my m__se safe from the __l. The __l lives on a tree near my h__se.

-ir, oo, er, ow, ou

It is my b__thday today. There will be all kinds of f__d to eat. Mother is getting a cake from the bak__y. The cl__n will come to perform at my h__se.

Let's Review

-ai-

-ay-

-ea-

-ee-

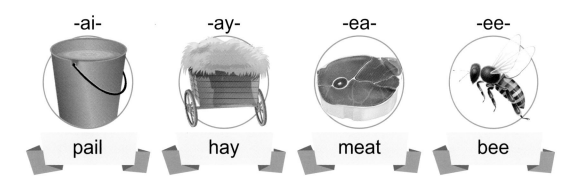

pail

hay

meat

bee

-oa-

-ow-

-oi-

-oy-

boat

row

coin

toy

-ou-

-ow-

-oo-

-oo-

mouse

owl

pool

cook

-ar-

-or-

-er-

-ir-

-ur-

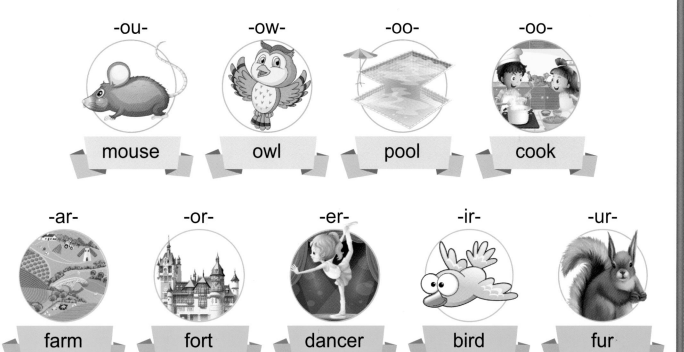

farm

fort

dancer

bird

fur

Write each word under its own picture.

oil, crown, pray, oyster, train, purse, sea, house, clerk, book, tree, food, park, skirt, toad, torch, snow

-ai-

-ay-

-ea-

-ee-

-oa-

-ow-

-oi-

-oy-

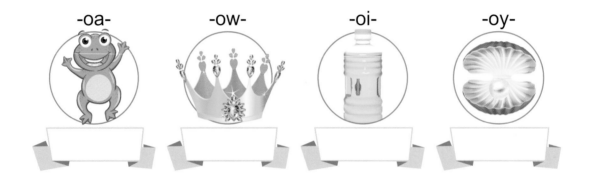

-ou-

-ow-

-oo-

-oo-

-ar-

-or-

-er-

-ir-

-ur-

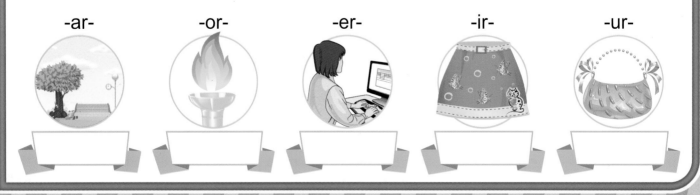

Match the Words

Read carefully the words written in the word box. Now look at the pictures and write the words under the right pictures.

Word Box
tray, tea, house, soap, rain
clown, boil, boy, snow

Hidden Words

Write the word for each picture.
Then find the words in the crossword.

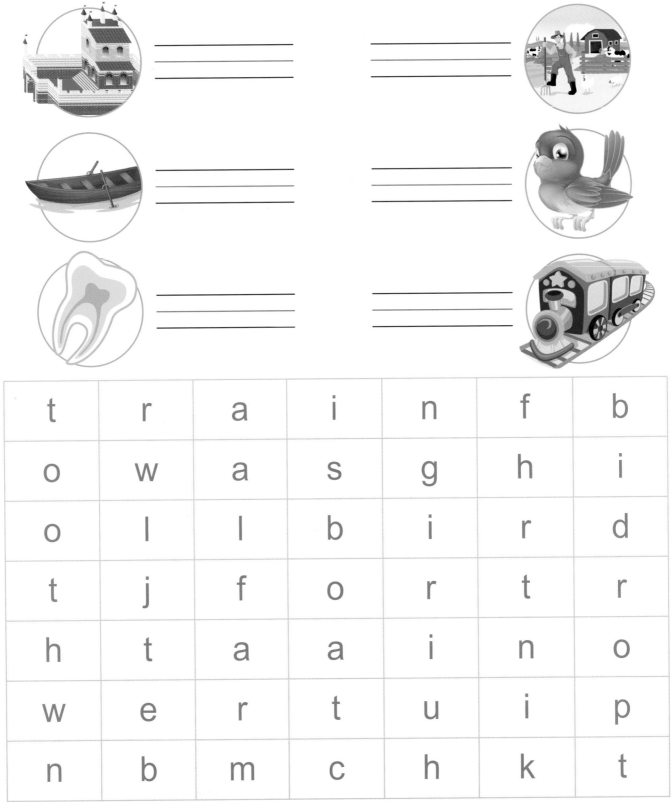

t	r	a	i	n	f	b
o	w	a	s	g	h	i
o	l	l	b	i	r	d
t	j	f	o	r	t	r
h	t	a	a	i	n	o
w	e	r	t	u	i	p
n	b	m	c	h	k	t

Can You Complete This?

Write the word with two-vowel blends for each sentence.
Look at the picture for clue.

1. Use _____ when you take bath.

2. Put on a _____ coat when it is cold.

3. The blue _____ caught a fly.

4. The _____ has seven colours.

5. Fill the_____ with water.

What Do You See?

Look at the pictures carefully. What do you see? Name and write the words with two-vowel blends that you see in this picture.

_____   _____   _____
_____   _____   _____
_____   _____   _____

             _____   _____
             _____   _____
             _____   _____

                          _____
                          _____
                          _____

94

Story Time

Use the words given in the word box to complete the story.
Look at the picture for clues.

One day, John was waiting for the _____. Suddenly, it began to _____ and a cold _____ started blowing. Soon, a nearby pond was filled with water and a green _____ began to croak. John saw some children dancing and jumping in the _____ and having a lot of _____ in the rain. They filled a _____ with water. John started feeling cold, so he took out his raincoat out from his bag and wore it. After some time, the train arrived and John boarded the train.

Word Box
train, breeze, toad, rain, park, fun, pail

Unscramble Us

Unscramble the letters to write the correct word in the blank.
Then match the word to its picture.

arpy _____

ehar _____

lolwip _____

nico _____

wnclo _____

ottoh _____

rcoth _____